AF292452

GUERNSEY SARK & HERM

A VIEW OF THE ISLANDS

CHRIS ANDREWS PUBLICATIONS
WITH GATEWAY PUBLISHING LTD SARK

First published in The Channel Islands in 2003 by
Chris Andrews Publications, Guernsey and Oxford
in association with Gateway Publishing Ltd Sark

Photographed and produced by Chris Andrews
Text Dallas Masterton
Design Mike Brain

All material © Chris Andrews
www. cap-ox.com

ISBN 0954033124

For copies of this book with your company logo and corporate
message or for picture library requests please contact
Chris Andrews Publications

Front cover Guernsey Harbour

Title page Cliffs at Les Tielles

ACKNOWLEDGEMENTS

Ginger Andrews, Duncan Spence, Jill and Gregg Vaudin.

Colour separations by Radstock Reproductions

Printed and bound in Great Britain by Butler and Tanner Ltd

Frome and London

CHRIS ANDREWS PUBLICATIONS
15 Curtis Yard North Hinksey Lane
Oxford OX2 0LX

Telephone: +44(0)1865 723404
email: chris.andrews1@btclick.com

G U E R N S E Y
S A R K & H E R M

A view of the Islands *by* Chris Andrews *text by* Dallas Masterton

CONTENTS

FOREWORD

From: His Excellency Lieutenant General Sir John Foley, KCB, OBE, MC

TELEPHONE:
01481 726666 (OFFICIAL)
01481 720002 (PRIVATE)

GOVERNMENT HOUSE,
GUERNSEY GY1 1GH,
CHANNEL ISLANDS.

FOREWORD

The outstanding coastline beauties of Guernsey, Sark and Herm are matched by the architectural heritage of mellow granite houses and peaceful rural lanes. The ancient and modern history of the islands left its imprint in many ways on their faces and this has been beautifully captured by the dazzling photographs in this book.

John Foley

INTRODUCTION

Guernsey, Sark and Herm make up part of the Bailiwick of Guernsey. All have an atmosphere that is particular to the Channel Islands, yet each is unique. Their histories and cultures are connected, yet each has retained its own distinct identity. Islanders are keen to maintain their independence, to preserve the natural beauty, culture and traditions of their Islands, yet are willing also to embrace change.

The charm of the Islands owes much to the sea. It is the sea which creates the boundaries, be it gentle sandy beaches, hidden caves and gullies, or rugged cliffs. It is the sea which defines the physical extent of each Island — but this concept is in itself challenging, for tides move in and out, sometimes gently, sometimes not, shorelines shift, seascapes redefine themselves. The sea provides many with a livelihood, yet sometimes threatens comfort and safety. Local folklore ties itself around the sea: tales of pirates and buccaneers, of trade and industry and of war and fortification. The maritime heritage of the Islands is celebrated on many levels. Pride is taken in the lifeboats, the lighthouses, the seaborne ambulance and rescue services.

Guernsey, Sark and Herm, the same, but historically, socially, culturally and physically different. Just as it should be. We are all shaped and moulded by our environment, just as we, in our turn, mould and shape that space. Through images and words, this book seeks to reveal the drifts of Island life. It seeks to uncover those moments and places that touch the spiritual and emotional landscapes of all who have walked and breathed here. It seeks to celebrate the vibrant and the subtle, the timeless and the shifting, the ever-changing moods and shades of meaning. It seeks to share the magic…

Herm.

Sark and Brecqhou.

St. Peter Port Harbour and the Town Church.

Harbour Dawn.

GUERNSEY

The second largest of the Channel Islands, Guernsey sits proudly in the Gulf of St. Malo in the Bay of Normandy. Described by Victor Hugo as "Fragments of France which fell into the sea and were picked up by England", the feeling this mixed parentage brings is unique, a mingling of relaxed Gallic insouciance and a sense of British orderliness creates an identity distinct from any other.

Originally part of the European land mass — high hills set above plains — the Channel Islands are now in the unique position of being close enough to France to see it, but part of the British Isles. The Bailiwick of Guernsey was originally part of the Duchy of Normandy. This changed in 1066 when Duke William of Normandy became King William I (William the Conqueror) of England, defeating King Harold at the Battle of Hastings. Hence today some Islanders argue that the British Isles are owned by Guernsey, not vice versa!

The Channel Islands today maintain independence in all local affairs — through their States of Deliberation, they are self-governing. The Queen is represented through the Lieutenant-Governor who may sit and speak in the States' Assembly, is in charge of military matters and who is present at most official occasions. In return for loyalty demonstrated in the past, British monarchs have continued to observe established laws, customs and liberties in the Bailiwick through a series of Royal Charters.

At one time the administrative unit in Guernsey was a "fief", governed by a seigneur, but the Island now works upon a parochial system. There are ten parishes in Guernsey: St. Peter Port, St. Sampson, Vale, Câtel, St. Andrews, St. Saviour, St. Martin, Forest, Torteval and St. Pierre du Bois. Each parish is represented in the States by a number of elected independent Deputies, and they each have a council, called a Douzaine, who are responsible for more parochial matters such as collecting rates and the bi-annual inspection of streams and hedges.

Parish boundary.

Guernsey south coast and the airport.

Alongside its own government, Guernsey has its own banknotes, postal system, and its own language. Guernsey patois, Guernesiaise, is a language based on Normandy French of some 900 years ago; it was the official language of the Island until 1921 when it was superseded by English. "Sarnia" as Guernsey is known in the local patois, translates as "Green Land". Although now heavily built up in some areas, there are still many places of natural beauty. The South Coast, stretching from Pleinmont to Jerbourg, boasts soaring cliffs and green headlands punctuated by small, sheltered coves. The landscape of the West Coast is lower and gentler, bays are more open here and often feature large rock formations. The beaches on this side of the Island are renowned for their good surfing, and occasionally the remains of an ancient forest can be seen breaching the sands of Vazon Bay. L'Ancresse and Pembroke Bays dominate the North Coast, sweeping across it with their wide expanses of pale sand. Inland there are historic buildings and working farms with stock.

The climate in Guernsey is generally milder than that of Mainland Britain, but strong winds, storms and sudden squalls are not uncommon. This has a practical effect upon many elements of Island life: dependent upon

The Golden Guernsey Goat - the breed preserved by secretly hiding a few pairs (from the table) during the war years.

Divette and the Pine Forest.

air and sea routes for numerous supplies and services, bad weather may mean that at some times, Islanders are, quite literally, marooned, with no outside mail or newspapers, no way of getting in and out. This may be the exception rather than the rule, but the cries of foghorns, like those of the gulls, are a reminder of the vulnerability of Island life.

The three main industries in Guernsey today are those of finance, horticulture and tourism. At one time the mild climate meant that Guernsey dominated the British tomato market, and large greenhouses remain a common sight. Today however, due to competition mainly from Holland, these are more likely to be filled with flowers – freesias, carnations and roses. In recent years the availability of cheap foreign travel has had a profound effect upon the Island's tourism industry. Fewer families visit the Island for their annual holiday, visitors today tend to come for short breaks, taking advantage of the mild weather and extended summer which the Island enjoys. Conferences, too, find Guernsey a pleasing venue, reflecting the Island's important role in the International Finance Industry. One of the most profound social and economic changes in Guernsey in recent years has been the development of Guernsey as an Offshore Banking Centre. The increasing numbers of large finance houses have changed the face of St. Peter Port and the coastal stretch along to Guernsey's second largest town, St. Sampson. Imposing stone and glass fronts of impressive proportions dominate the Town seafront and rise to punctuate the skyline: monuments again to the ability of the people of Guernsey not only to nurture continuity, but to respond to change.

Top: Cranes project above the traditional rooftops.
Bottom: One of the new buildings.

Former tomato vinery now used for floral production only.

ST PETER PORT

St. Peter Port began as a small fishing village. There was no natural harbour here — the shelter offered by the lay of the land and the other islands gave it the opportunity to grow. Fishing encouraged the development of other trades like boatbuilding, and rope and net making. The harbour was on the main European trading routes and was often used to escape foul weather and replenish stores. So traders and merchants also contributed to the growth from village to the principle town in the Island. In the Eighteenth and Nineteenth Centuries, the wine trade flourished, as a tax free port with no duties to be paid, merchants saw opportunities here for expansion. Wine was laid down to mature in the cellars and vaults of the town. Buildings which now host prestigious finance houses may feature unusually shaped windows — their curved tops bearing witness to this past, these were the original wine vaults.

Not only is St. Peter Port the capital of Guernsey and home to the Island's government, it remains the main port of entry from the sea. It is also the centre of the Island's finance industry, though some of the larger institutions have been forced to move their operations to the outskirts of Town in order to expand. St. Peter Port is Guernsey's main shopping area, and, like any other bustling, cosmopolitan town, is also home for many people. Part of St. Peter Port's charm lies in the way all of these roles are played out in buildings which have had previous lives. The elegant Regency Town houses of the wealthy have become the shops and restaurants of today; the workhouse built in 1742 is now the Police Station; the renowned concert hall of St. James was a church built in 1818 to provide services for the English speaking garrison stationed in Guernsey.

Until the Eighteenth Century the town was compact. Relying still on fishing and activities related to it, the economic and commercial life of St. Peter Port was conducted along the waterfront and in Fountain Street, Cornet Street, La Grande Rue (the High Street), La Rue des Forges (Smith Street) and Le Pollet.

Stained glass in St. James.

The houses in Lower Vauvert wind down the hill so steeply that they seem to be stacked one upon the other. In the Regency period the road was widened to reduce the danger to children from passing carts.

17

These streets, known as "Old Town" continue to form the hub of the town. "New Town" came into existence during the Eighteenth Century, built upon the phenomenal profits of Privateering. New wealth attracted new residents. So came the building of the elegant Georgian suburbs around Elizabeth College, itself part of this expansion, built in 1826. Many of the streets here bear the names of the people who gave the land over to be built upon: De Havilland Street, Allez Street, Sausmarez Street.

The High Street is the main artery of the town. A thoroughfare which once rang with the hooves of horses and carriage wheels (it is difficult to imagine how two carriages would have passed alongside each other), the High Street is, with slight exceptions, pedestrianised. Little alleyways, or "venelles" run down to the Esplanade and quays and the town is as bustling and energetic as it would have been when these were filled with merchants, seamen and porters carrying goods to and from the ships which sat in the harbour. The High Street is bounded at one end by the Town Church. Developing from a fishermens' chapel, the written records of the church date back to 1048. The colours of the Royal Guernsey Militia hang in the sanctuary and at one time, the north aisle housed the parish fire pump. The Town Church also boasts the curious distinction of being the closest church to a pub in the British Isles. A stone gargoyle stretches towards the pub and there is barely a metre between them — evidence perhaps not only of the differing central points around which society revolves, but the necessity for both.

The growth continued. No longer able to house either the residents or economic activity of a bustling Victorian age, St. Peter Port spread further up the hill. The areas around Candie and Hauteville were developed. Large Town Houses were built. That of Osmond de Beauvoir Priaulx now hosts the Priaulx Library, and the grounds made way for the building of the Guernsey Museum in 1978. Another was demolished in 1972 to allow for the construction of Beau Sejour Leisure Centre which opened in1976. Victor Hugo, the French writer and philanthropist who was exiled in Guernsey from 1855 to 1870, occupied a large Victorian mansion in Hauteville which he made very distinctly his own. The whole town of St. Peter Port bore witness to the industry and enterprise of the period.

Today, "Town" as it is generally known, is still the vital and pulsing centre of much of Island life. The waterfront is a vibrant collage of

yachts and ferries, funnels and rigging. The marinas created to provide moorings for visiting sea craft, appear to have extended the boundaries of St. Peter Port, taking them out onto the water. The quayside, created from reclaimed land between 1775 and 1779 to prevent the incursion of the sea at the entrances to the houses, seems now to sit between tall stately buildings and a constantly shifting and changing sea of colour and activity.

The quayside and inner harbour.

Harbour, Herm and Jethou at dawn.

The breakwater, joining Castle Cornet to mainland Guernsey, was completed in 1859. The lighthouse on the end, now a popular fishing spot, first shone its light in 1867.

The Town and harbour from Fort George.

White Rock Pier, first used for landing passengers by the Southampton packets in 1864, now houses customs buildings, ferry terminals, and offices for various shipping agents.

Dusk, the harbour entrance and the Town.

Bathers and the pools at Havelet Bay.

The annual Castle Swim from the bathing pools to Castle Cornet.

Visitors and locals in the harbour.

*Many uniquely local shops and restaurants line
the busy Town streets.*

The Royal Court House 1799, houses the States of Deliberation,
the Royal Court Chamber and the public records office, the Greffe.

Floral Guernsey: a display on the busy embankment at
"The Bankers Draught," public house.

Castle Cornet, a military installation almost constantly manned since 1206. At high tide the sea washes empty limpet shells against the wall and the little enclosed beach echoes with an etherial tinkle.

Christmas in Town.

Candie Gardens, originally the gardens of Osmond de Beauvoir Priaulx who bequeathed them to the people of Guernsey. In addition to spectacular floral displays the gardens house what are believed to be Guernsey's first glasshouses, as well as statues of Victor Hugo and Queen Victoria.

Interior of the flower and vegetable market.

The House and statue of Victor Hugo
The statue of Hugo in Candie Gardens bears the inscription
from the dedication of "The Toilers of the Sea":

Au rocher d'hospitalité et de liberté,
à ce coin de vieille terre, Normande
où vit le noble petit people de la mer
à l'Ile de Guernsey, sévère et douce.

("To the rock of hospitality and liberty, to this corner of ancient
Norman soil, where live the noble little people of the sea, to the
Island of Guernsey, stern and gentle.")

Rooftops. St. James' Concert and Assembly Hall and Elizabeth College were both designed by the architect John Wilson in the Nineteenth Century. Old Government House Hotel is in the foreground.

A street at the top of Town.

The Victorian Pillar Box in Union Street dates from 1852-53. It is the oldest surviving example of the early roadside posting boxes installed by the Post Office, and remains in use today.

The cobbled slipway behind the Model Yacht Pond with the lighthouse at the end of Castle Pier.

Cargo vessel and cruise liner pass in the water known as
The Little Russel between Herm and Guernsey.

Fermain Bay, the Eighteenth Century Loophole Tower
known colloquially as "The Pepper Pot."

Fermain Bay: Fermain is the Breton word meaning "strong rock". The bay can be approached by way of the green wooded paths from St. Peter Port or Jerbourg Point.

Divette Pier, Marble Bay and the coast looking back to St. Peter Port.

Majestic rocks off the south coast.

Sausmarez Manor, Guernsey's only stately home.
Attractions in the grounds include a sculpture trail.

The Entrance Hall. For centuries members of the de Sausmarez family have held prominent
positions in Guernsey government, the British Foreign Office and the Royal Navy.

Petit Bôt, with one of the Island's smallest beaches.

Saints Bay.

*Le Gouffre translates as "The Gulf". A steep cliff path
leads down to the small harbour at La Moye Point.*

View west from Le Gouffre, and Greater Black Back Gull.

Forest Parish Church is the smallest parish church in the Island. During the Occupation it was closed, believed to be too close to the airport. Attendance would have posed too great a threat.

Cliff flowers including the characteristic Sea Thrift at Les Tielles.

Rue des Vinaires, St. Pierre du Bois.

Spring in St. Pierre du Bois.

Portelet Pier and Rocquaine Bay.

Portelet Bay.

Route de la Rocque. The shingle banks which form a barrier to the sea, the seashore at L'Eree and the marsh here are part
of a conservation area. It is an important breeding ground and stop off point for migrating birds.

Fort Grey, originally known as Chateau de Rocquaine, and reputed to be the haunt of witches. Today however, it is better known for its Maritime Museum.

Watermill in Rue de Quanteraine, St. Pierre du Bois.

The Orchid Fields at L'Eree contain many specimens of British loose-flowered orchids. "Pougencoute" in Guernsey patois, the orchids are named after the season in which they flower: Pentecost.

L'Eree Bay and Lihou Island. A causway, passable at low tide, connects the Island to Guernsey.

Rocquaine Bay looking towards Fort Saumarez.

The church of St. Saviour is the largest of Guernsey's parish churches. The lanes around the church are particularly characteristic.

*The Little Chapel at Les Vauxbelets
built in 1923 by two French monks,
Brother Deodat and Brother Cephas.
Modelled on the shrine at Lourdes, at
16ft long it is one of the smallest
churches in the world.*

Vazon Bay.

Fort Hommet.

Vazon

The west coast is known for a spectacular variety of sunsets, this one at Cobo.

Cobo Bay

Port Soif.

Portinfer.

74

Grande Havre Bay sweeps round from Chouet to Rousse Tower.

Vale Church is believed to have been on this site for about 1000 years. Before the draining of the Braye (a stretch of sea water dividing the parish) some wishing to attend worship had to travel by rowing boat.

L'Ancresse.

The Bay stretches between Fort Le Marchant and Fort Pembroke.

78

*Guernsey's first yacht marina, Beaucette. Once a quarry, the granite barrier
to the sea was blasted out by the Marines to create the entrance.*

*Oysters, one of Guernsey's principle exports in the
1820s, are now being farmed in St. Sampson.*

The Neolithic passage grave of the Dehus Dolmen at Bordeaux. The stones in the roof at the end of the chamber are carved with the hands and face of a bearded man —"The Guardian"— said to be holding a bow and arrow.

The Chapel of St. Apolline 1392. Once used as a stable it became
Guernsey's first designated and protected ancient monument in 1873.

Bordeaux Harbour where Hugo sited Gilliat's haunted house in "The Toilers of the Sea",
beyond is Vale Castle and the entrance to St. Sampson's harbour.

Before the draining of the Braye du Valle and the reclamation of the land in 1806, the Vale Castle would have occupied a strategic site. It now looks out over the Ronez Cement Works.

84

*St. Sampson, a working port and Guernsey's second largest
shopping centre, situated in the north of the Island.*

St. Sampson's Harbour before the controversial Marina development. The inner harbour is protected by the Crocq jetty with its clock tower and an obelisk erected in 1872.

The Island from the west.

A variety of buildings and spectacular floral displays, typical of the Island.

SARK

Sark lies eight miles to the east of Guernsey, a rocky plateau some three hundred feet high of irregular shape, broadly three miles long and one and a half miles wide. Whilst there are some beaches and sheltered bays, the coastline is predominantly sheer cliff. The Island can be reached only by the sea, the crossing taking about 45 minutes from Guernsey's St. Peter Port, passing Herm, Jethou and the remarkable Gothic style castle on Brecqhou.

Sark's magnificent coastline gives no clue to the the country above, of small green fields with here and there thickly wooded valleys leading to bays or coves. The Island has an air of peace and retains an old world charm, doubtless helped by the absence of cars. Travel is by foot, bicycle or horse (and carriage); there is one public transport, the "Toast Rack" which brings people up the steep Harbour Hill. Tractors are used for agricultural or other heavy work.

The feudal system established by the first Seigneur continues to form the basis for Sark's legal and political system. Although part of Guernsey's Bailiwick, Sark is self-governing. Recent change by the Island has brought many of its laws up to date but it manages well without an excess of intrusive legislation.

The Island's main industries today are tourism, fishing, farming and some limited financial enterprises. In the distant past Sark was involved in mining; the remains of the mines are still to be seen on Little Sark. La Coupée, a narrow isthmus joining Sark and Little Sark is perhaps the most dramatic of the Island's many impressive features.

Sark has long attracted visitors. In the Eighteenth Century weekend parties from Guernsey became an established practice. In the Nineteenth Century the island became popular with Victorian artists, poets and writers, including J.M.W. Turner who made La Coupée the subject of a drawing, Victor Hugo, for whom some caves were named, and the writer Mervyn Peake, whose novel "Mr Pye" was filmed on the Island during the 1980's.

*Sark cuisine at
The Aval du Creux Hotel.*

Ferry heading to Maseline Harbour.

Creux, said to be one of the smallest harbours in the world.

The east side of the Island, Creux and Maseline harbours, and
the hill to the centre.

Creux is a working harbour, much used by
local fishermen and visitors alike

The Bon Marin off the Bec du Nez, on a lively day.

Dixcart and Derrible from the south.

Early evening on Dixcart Beach.

La Coupée, connecting
Little Sark to Big Sark.

One of several canons still left on the Island,
this one before and above La Coupée.

Port Gorey and remains of The Silver Mine.

A dairy herd walks to the parlour in Rue du Fort.

*The Gouliot Caves contain an
extraordinary variety of marine life.*

Gouliot Headland and the west coast.

The Moie de Mouton on the west coast.

Carriages at St. Peters, the Island's Anglican Church.

The Seigneurie.

The Chelsea Pensioners visit the gardens.

Equipment shed at the Seigneurie working farm.

Wild garlic.

Stone carved by a Buddhist Monk on the Eperquerie.

Brecqhou.

The combination of sun and wind bleach dead timber.

*Snow is rare, though this time, in April was perhaps
even more unusual.*

*Flowers on Sark, both wild and cultivated, are
renowned for their colour and variety.*

Colour and contrast in a carriage.

Summer, and the annual Lord's Taverners charity cricket match.

Winter, the fishing gear laid up.

HERM

Herm lies about three miles to the east of Guernsey. It is only one and a half miles long by three quarters of a mile wide, yet visitors to the island feel that here time itself has been stretched out. Perhaps it is the peacefulness, the calmness, the quiet – the name itself is said to mean "deserted land". Whatever the special quality is, time spent on Herm is to be savoured slowly.

After a series of private tenants, including the writer Compton Mackenzie who also leased Jethou, Herm was purchased from the Crown in 1946 for the sum of £15,000. Leased out to the Wood family by the States of Guernsey since 1949, Herm has been developed in a way that maximizes the Island's resources without impinging on its natural charm and beauty. Dependent for much of its income on tourism, the old farm cottages have been renovated to provide holiday accommodation, campsites have been established and amenities provided, and the hotel modernized. Day-trippers are well catered for, as Herm village has shops as well as a tavern and restaurant. There is a working farm, a manor house, the small yet beautiful St. Tugual's chapel, and many delightful walks and beaches.

Whilst known for many years as the playground for the Governors of Guernsey and their guests, Herm's long history reveals a more important role. It is believed that Herm was originally a burial ground for French kings – prehistoric remains and artefacts unearthed show them to be too many for the size of community that would have existed in Herm. Monks inhabited the island at various periods of its history, as late as the 1880s. Quarrying became important in Herm in the 1830s and there was also a largely unsuccessful copper mine, above Rosaire.

Herm is not just a holiday island. It is very much a community. It has its own school, power station, fire service and even a prison – one of the smallest in the world. For both residents and visitors alike, Herm, with its beautiful beaches, proliferation of bird life, profusion of wild flowers and general air of calm and well-being, has what Jenny Wood called, a "magical appeal".

The way over.

The quayside, for both passengers and cargo.

The harbour.

Trident heading back to Guernsey. At low tide the many hazardous rocks dictate a more circuitous route.

Jethou is privately owned, and it is the place where Compton Mackenzie wrote "Whiskey Galore" and "Fairy Gold". The two outlying rocks show navigation markers.

Herm and Jethou from Guernsey at sunrise.

The Manor House, altered significantly and crenellations
added by the tenant of 1889 - 1915, Prince Blucher.

Herm is noted for the beauty of its wild flowers. Extensive work is carried out on both wild and cultivated floral displays. The Island has earned many Gold Awards at Floral Guernsey and Britain in Bloom.

Sea Pinks on the coastline leading to Shell Beach.

Shell Beach is one of the principle Island attractions. There are said to be over 200 varieties of shells washed up by the passing Gulf Stream, some from as far away as the Gulf of Mexico.

Fisherman's Beach, with the village, harbour and Jethou.

View from Le Petit Monceau towards Guernsey. Situated on Herm Common, Le Petit Monceau has large flat stones which may have come from Neolithic graves.

The Island has a herd of about forty beef cattle.

The White House and its award winning gardens.

Belvoir Bay, a popular beach with its sands sloping into the clear water, sits in the foreground. Shell Beach can be seen behind.

The Island from the south-east.

The Mermaid Tavern, an integral part of any visit.

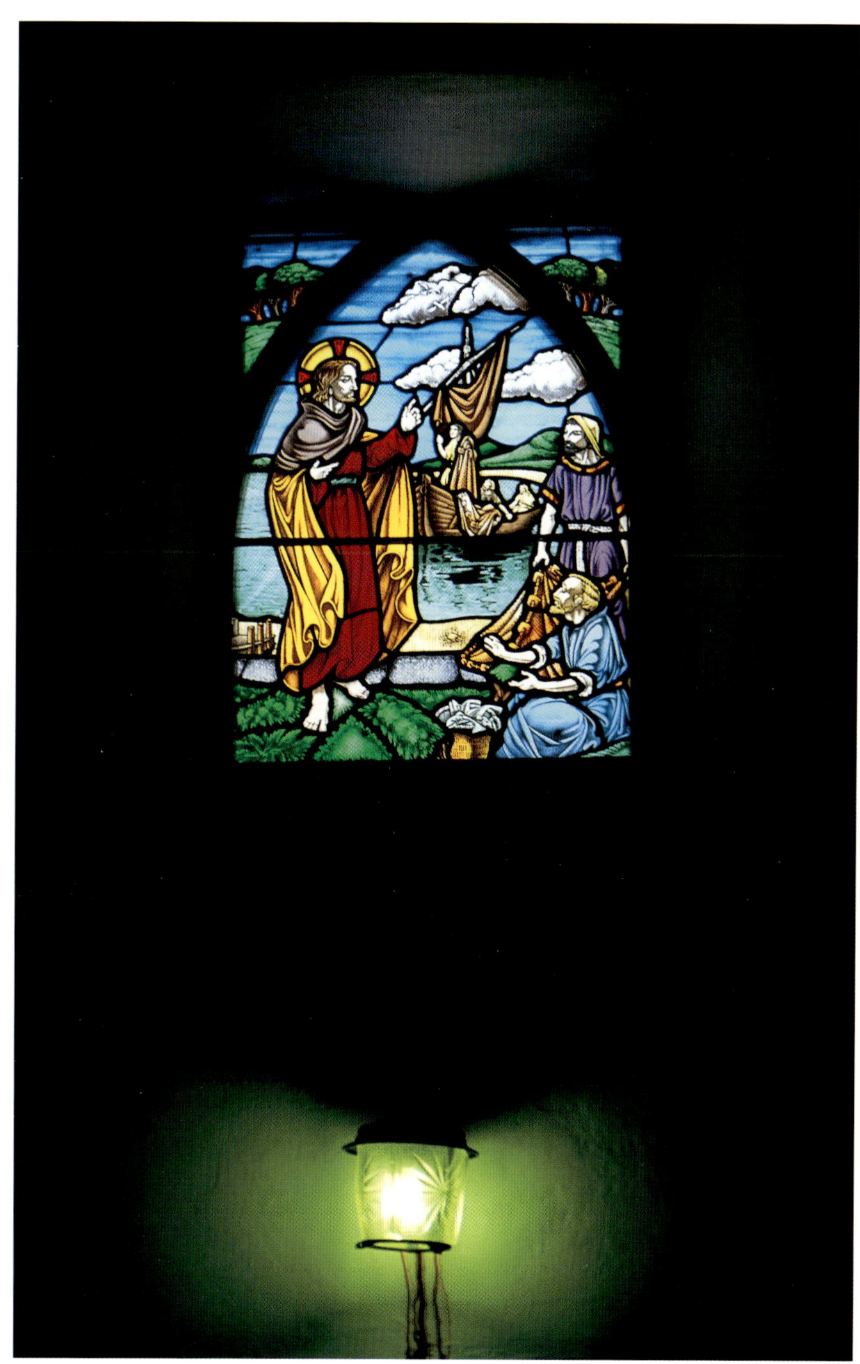

*Herm was once a religious outpost. One theory
is that St. Tugual was a Welsh woman who
accompanied St. Magliore to Guernsey and
Herm in the Sixth Century. St. Tugual's Chapel
is still used for regular worship on Sundays.
Visitors who wish to take part in the service
are encouraged to do so. Sir Cliff Richard is
one well-known Christian who took the
opportunity, leading in song and prayer.*

Practice rescue with the Flying Christine, off Mouisonniere Beach.

Time to leave.

ISLAND LIFE

The pulling power of Sark; Jurats on the Quayside;
Majorettes at The Battle of Flowers; Liberation Day visit.

The sea wall, Vazon.

The walk to work in Town and show jumping at L'Eree.

At The Liberation Monument; The West Show;
Hand milking; summer in the surf.

Benches at The Town Church.

Fish and chips on the sea wall at Cobo; end of the day in Sark;
outdoor school Sark; and open air theatre at Castle Cornet.

"Fragments of France
which fell into the sea
and were picked up by
England".

Victor Hugo